**Ludvigsen Library Series**

CORVETTE
The Exotic Experimental Cars

Introduction by
Karl Ludvigsen

Iconografix

Iconografix
PO Box 446
Hudson, Wisconsin 54016 USA

Library of Congress Card Number: 99-76046

ISBN 1-58388-017-8

00 01 02 03 04 05 06 5 4 3 2 1

Printed in the United States of America

Cover and book design by Shawn Glidden

Copy Editing by Dylan Frautschi

Iconografix Inc. exists to preserve history through the publication of notable photographic archives and the list of titles under the Iconografix imprint is constantly growing. Transportation enthusiasts should be on the Iconografix mailing list and are invited to write and ask for a catalog, free of charge.

Authors and editors in the field of transportation history are invited to contact the Editorial Department at Iconografix, Inc., PO Box 446, Hudson, WI 54016. We require a minimum of 120 photographs per subject. We prefer subjects narrow in focus, e.g., a specific model, railroad, or racing venue. Photographs must be of high quality, suited to large format reproduction.

ACKNOWLEDGMENTS

The photos in this book are from the Ludvigsen Library in London, England, which may be contacted by e-mail at library@ludvigsen.com. Over the years some photos were gathered from the files of GM Styling/Design in the course of Mr. Ludvigsen's writings about Corvettes. Some are Mr. Ludvigsen's own photos, for example of the CERV II and Corvette 2-Rotor. The photos of the 1953 Corvette at Paris and Brussels were taken by Rudy Mailander, whose negatives are held by the Library. Also included are photos from the personal archives of Zora Arkus-Duntov and Larry Shinoda.

INTRODUCTION

The prototype that led to my deepest involvement with Corvettes was Bill Mitchell's racing Sting Ray of 1959. Driven by the 'flying dentist' from Washington, D.C., Dr. Dick Thompson, the Sting Ray was the SCCA Class C Modified champion racer of 1960. When I saw Dick herding it around the fast, bumpy Bridgehampton track on May 30, 1960, I was stunned by the speed and capability of the metallic silver Sting Ray. Many observers had tended to ignore it because it wasn't made by some exotic Italian or German car company.

As the editor of *Car and Driver* I exercised my prerogative and scheduled and wrote a technical report, with cutaway drawing by Clarence LaTourette, on this amazing car. It was published in our March 1961 issue. Unbeknownst to me, the Sting Ray's creator, GM Styling chief Bill Mitchell, was on the lookout for a public relations person who could help him communicate the huge and refreshing enthusiasm for cars that he was bringing to Styling Staff after taking over from Harley Earl at the end of the 1950s. To make a long story short, he liked our Sting Ray article and I found myself hired by the GM Public Relations Staff at the end of 1961 and assigned to work with Bill and his colleagues at the glorious Saarinen-designed Technical Center in Warren, Michigan.

Five years earlier I had been peripherally involved with the steps that led to the creation of the 1957 Corvette SS, the car whose test chassis was used as the basis of the Sting Ray. I had worked for a few months in Styling's Research Studio in the summer of 1956. When I arrived, what did I find in the studio but a D-Type Jaguar! Our engineers were measuring its engine bay to see if they could fit in a Chevy V-8. Harley Earl's plan was to restyle the Chevy-engined Jaguar and race it at Sebring as an experimental Corvette. Whether he was bluffing or not we may never know, but this was the impetus that led to Chevrolet's decision to build the Corvette SS that raced – all too briefly – at Sebring in 1957.

Speaking of the SS, I was technical editor at *Sports Cars Illustrated* when reports of this new car began coming in early in 1957. Luckily I had a 'mole' at Chevrolet Engineering who could walk right into the shop where it was being built and tell me all about it (Where are you now, John Camden?). This gave us at *SCI* an exceptionally authoritative slant on this important new car.

That summer of 1956, when I first worked at Styling, I saw the models of the four-headlight Corvette that was launched in 1958. Bill Mitchell was ebullient about this new design, styled in the baroque manner then typical of GM. "Just like a Cadillac!" he exclaimed about this chrome-laden car. Some of us had our doubts. But it was a good Corvette and it matured into the handsome 1961 model with its bevelled tail. I picked one of these up in Detroit well before the official release date and drove it east to be subjected to a full Road Research Report in *Car and Driver*.

While still at *C/D* I had a chance to drive the 'Blue Car,' Zora Arkus-Duntov's test mule for the all-new 1963 Corvette. Clad in 1962 model body panels, it had the full 1963 chassis under the skin. With its stunning rear traction and grip it was a revelation, a huge step ahead of the old live-axle chassis. I recall driving it around the same time as the first Jaguar XK-E; clearly we were entering a promising new era in the engineering of production sports cars.

One of the first artifacts I saw when I arrived at GM at the end of 1961 was the styling model of the production Stingray and, as well, the model of the stretched 2+2 version that Chevrolet chief Ed Cole had lobbied for. This (obviously) didn't go into production, but it left its mark in Stingray frame rails that were heavier than they needed to be.

Behind the scenes I helped with the press launch of the Stingray, putting together packs of photos of the creation of the new car and comparison photos of the road car with the racer that inspired it. I also had the privilege of driving one of the spanking-new 1963 coupes down to Watkins Glen in September 1962 for the US Grand Prix. Just starting its Total Performance push, Ford was showing off its mid-engined Mustang at the Glen and we at GM wanted to do all we could to upstage the Blue Oval gang. Wherever it went at the Grand Prix the Stingray was a sensation. I practically wore out the battery demonstrating the hidden headlights.

Before leaving the original Sting Ray racer, I have to mention that a major perk of my GM job was the chance to demonstrate this wonderful car to visiting firemen. Sometimes Bill Mitchell would do that himself, as he did when engineer Rudy Uhlenhaut of Mercedes-Benz came to lunch. A few laps around the reflecting pool at the heart of the Tech Center were wonderfully invigorating. With its injected engine and locked rear end, the Sting Ray was mighty quick and a delight to drive. One day when I brought it rumbling back to the Styling garage one of the mechanics said, "You love driving that, don't you?" I'll say!

Soon after the launch of the production Stingray, but before Christmas of 1962, Zora took me to a small, windowless room accessed from one of the back corridors of the Chevy Engineering Center. There I saw for the first time the frame and suspension components of the incredible Corvette Grand Sport. Planned for a production run of 125 cars, this ultra-light tube-framed Corvette coupe would have had a 16-plug engine of 550+ horsepower and Cobra-eating performance. But a reaffirmation of GM's anti-racing policy halted the production line at only five cars.

The early 1960s were the years when Frank Winchell and his 'skunk works' at Chevrolet Engineering were beginning to experiment with new chassis designs using both Corvair and Corvette engines and components. Theirs was the work that led to the epic cooperation with Jim Hall and Chaparral and the advancement of the art of the sports-racing car. One of the engineers working with Frank was the talented Jim Musser; inevitably one of his prototypes would be dubbed the 'Musserati.' It was the test-mule version of the gorgeous Corvair Monza GT.

When body designs were needed for these oddball prototypes, they would be modeled by Studio X in the Styling Staff cellar. Ed Wayne was the studio chief, Tony Lapine the engineer, and Larry Shinoda the designer. They created the exotic shape of the CERV I, Zora's 1960 single-seater built originally to make an attack on the outright record for the Pike's Peak hill climb. Although Zora practiced at the Peak – he showed me his home movies of his tests there – the attempt was never made.

I was at Riverside at the end of 1960 when the spectacular CERV I took some demonstration laps before the Grand Prix in the hands of Stirling Moss. Dan Gurney had test-driven it at Riverside as well. Later the CERV I was groomed for closed-course record-breaking; Zora lapped GM's Milford, Michigan high-speed track at a stunning 206 mph average. But it never had a chance to strut its stuff officially.

Another CERV – Chevrolet Engineering Research Vehicle – was built in 1964 as a basis for a Chevrolet counterattack to Ford's commitment to endurance racing with the GT40. The CERV II, as it was named, was and is a hugely innovative car with four-wheel drive from a mid-placed engine, using tailored torque converters to drive the front and rear axles. Each axle also had a two-speed gearbox so the car could be operated in high and low speed ranges.

Built initially as an open roadster, the CERV II was first tested in complete secrecy in 1964. Years later, in November 1970 to be specific, it came to public attention as a result of the initiative of your author. At that time

Motor Trend and *Sports Car Graphic* were sister magazines in the Petersen stable. One morning the editor of *Sports Car Graphic* stepped into the office of his technical editor, a former Chevrolet R&D engineer.

"What do you know about the CERV II?" he innocently asked the engineer.

"Well," came the hesitant response, "it's still secret. I don't know how much I can tell you about it."

"*Damn it,*" the editor shouted, "*It's on the cover of this month's* Motor Trend!"

MT's editor Eric Dahlquist and I had struck again. We loved digging out the exotic stories and surprising our readers as well as the opposition. We published a complete description of this Corvette prototype and my driving impressions of the car on the Tech Center's check road. It didn't half haul. "Zero to 60 in 2.8 seconds," we said on the *MT* cover, and it certainly felt like it. The only thing I didn't try (on Zora's advice, and I still regret taking it) was upshifting the clutchless two-speed box.

Eric and I kept the momentum going with our exclusive in-depth stories in *Motor Trend* on the new generation of rotary-engined Corvettes unveiled at the end of 1973. The beautiful little Corvette 2-Rotor, fabricated for display purposes by Pininfarina on a Porsche 914 platform, was the car John De Lorean tried to persuade GM to release to him for production after he left the Corporation. As for the 4-Rotor, well, that was just stunning. I was on hand when it was completed and also when it was displayed in Europe.

These are just a few of the enjoyable recollections that I was afforded by this trawl through our archives in search of pictures of exotic Corvette prototypes and experimental cars over two decades. I hope you enjoy this look behind the Chevrolet Curtain at some of the most interesting designs from what was, in retrospect, a hugely creative period of car making.

Karl Ludvigsen
Islington, London
July, 1999

Europe's first sight of the production Corvette was at the Paris Salon in October 1953. Behind its protective grilles are special European headlamps.

Under the glass roof of the Grand Palais in Paris, the 1953 Corvette looked gorgeous in Polo White. Here was an American car to which Europeans could relate.

Under the hood of the Corvette displayed in Paris was the much-improved Chevrolet six of 235.5 cubic inches, its three Carter carburetors helping it develop 150 bhp at 4,200 rpm.

A transparent hood panel allowed visitors to admire the Corvette's six-cylinder engine when it was displayed at Brussels, Belgium in January 1954.

Zora Arkus-Duntov, behind the wheel, conducted high-speed tests at GM's Phoenix Proving Ground in 1955 on a V-8-engined 1954 Corvette prototype. He achieved 163 mph.

Zora's Phoenix tests established the configuration of the three Corvettes that raced on the beach at Daytona, Florida in 1956. From left to right the drivers were Betty Skelton, Zora, and John Fitch.

In early 1954 a proposal for a Corvette facelift adopted mock fender side vents and a Ferrari-like grille similar to that of the 1955 Chevrolet.

At the rear, the 1954 facelift proposal had a hooded license plate housing inspired by the tail of the Corvette-based "Corvair" coupe shown at the 1954 Motorama.

Although the baroque front and rear details of this 1957 Corvette styling proposal were not adopted, its side cove was an attractive feature of the 1957 model.

NADEL
4-11-55

10899

Liking the looks of the sports-car market, designers for GM's Buick Division proposed a two-seat roadster based on the Corvette chassis.

BT – NM
3-26-56

13451

For Sweden's Prince Bertil, a great car enthusiast, GM built this very special 1956 Corvette. Chrome rear-deck strips foreshadow the 1958 model.

The special Corvette for Prince Bertil had wire wheels, an altered grille, and European headlamps.

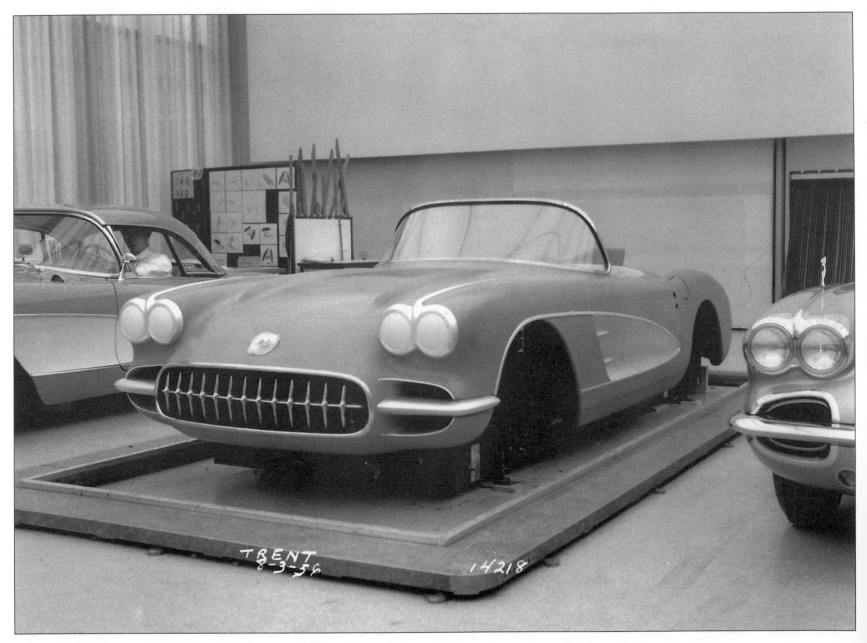

Designed after styling was complete on the 1958 model, this August 1956 Corvette proposal was aimed at a special competition version with its rear-deck fin. It was never built.

Behind an early styling proposal for the 1958 Corvette is a model with a quite different look, patterned after the Oldsmobile Golden Rocket Motorama car.

Belying its exaggerated looks, the SR-2 Corvette of 1957 was a serious competition car. It raced at Daytona, Sebring, and Road America.

20

GM stylists did not stint on the appearance of the interiors of their special Corvettes. This features twin windscreens, extra gauges, and a fire extinguisher.

A look behind the scenes at Sebring in 1957 finds the SR-2 up on stands for attention to its rear suspension. One of the more standard Corvettes behind it finished in 12th place in the 12-hour race.

Zora Duntov fitted a special tach and additional gauges, as well as a seat side bolster to the Corvette he drove to a timed average of 150.593 mph at Daytona in January 1956.

When GM's stylists were given an opportunity to design an all-out racing Corvette in 1956, they did not lack for ideas. It was dubbed project XP-64 by Styling Staff.

Styling concepts explored for the XP-64 (later named the Corvette SS) included clear grille identification with the standard Corvette and an unique circular headrest.

By September 1956 the shape of the XP-64 was being developed full-size in clay in the Chevrolet Studio at the GM Technical Center in Warren, Michigan.

As engineered by Zora Arkus-Duntov, the 1957 Corvette SS was a fully-realized sports-racing car taking advantage of the best engineering techniques then available. Its body was made of ultra-light magnesium.

TRENT
12-6-56

14987

Styling staff executive Ken Pickering lends a sense of scale to the model of the XP-64, compared here to a production Corvette fitted with Dayton wire wheels. The racing car's aerodynamic drag was similar to that of a D-Type Jaguar.

A special magnesium oil pan for the Chevy V-8 in the Corvette SS helped the engine weigh 80 pounds less than standard. Skilled fabrication of all frame and suspension components is evident.

Weighing 180 pounds with all its brackets, the tubular space frame of the Corvette SS was patterned after the successful design of the Mercedes-Benz 300SL. Large, tubular crossmembers were used at both front and rear between the coil spring abutments.

No sports-racing car ever had a more elegant instrument panel than the Corvette SS. Its rear-view mirror was integrated into the body design. A clock was useful for the endurance races for which the car was intended.

From parts supposedly intended for a static mock-up, Zora and his crew built a second Corvette SS to serve as a test "mule." This fiberglass-bodied car was extensively tested before Sebring in 1957.

Zora himself wheels the SS out of its garage at Sebring in 1957, its side panels removed to try to reduce the high cockpit temperatures. In the race the car completed only 23 laps.

Capable of averaging 183 mph around GM's Phoenix Proving Ground track, Zora and the SS are here lapping at 155 mph during the official opening of the Daytona International Speedway in February 1959.

After becoming head of GM Styling in December 1958, Bill Mitchell obtained the "mule" chassis of the Corvette SS. It was clothed in the magnificent body of the original Sting Ray, which was every inch a real racing car.

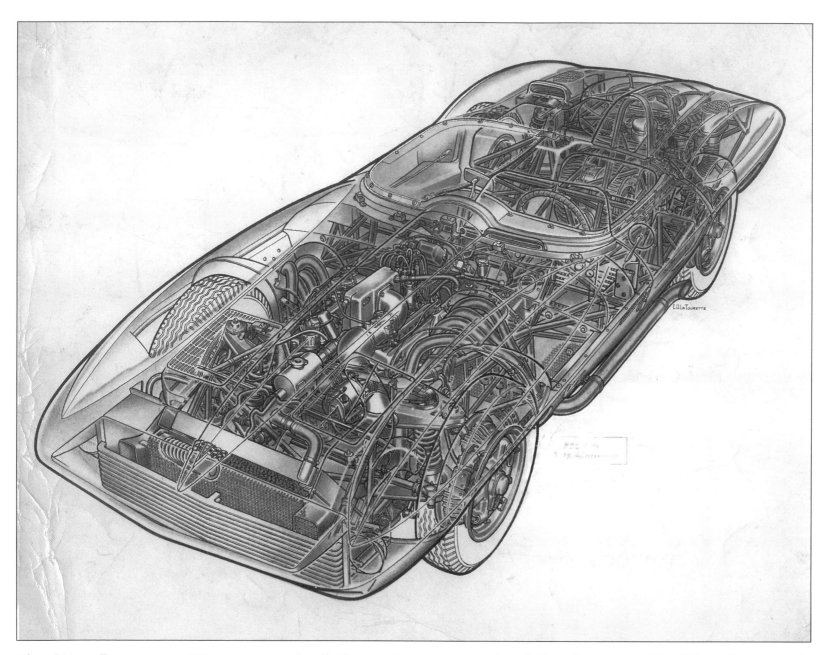

The Sting Ray competition car used all the main components of the Corvette SS, although a much simplified braking system contributed to improved performance. Brakes were mounted inboard at the rear.

Doctor Richard Thomson drove the Silver Sting Ray to the SCCA Class C Modified championship in 1960. At Cumberland, Maryland he is avoiding the pirouetting Porsche of Bob Holbert.

After its racing career ended, the Sting Ray was fitted with disc brakes, a 427-cubic-inch Chevy V-8 topped by Weber carburetors, and a transparent air scoop. Mechanic Ken Eschebach is at the wheel.

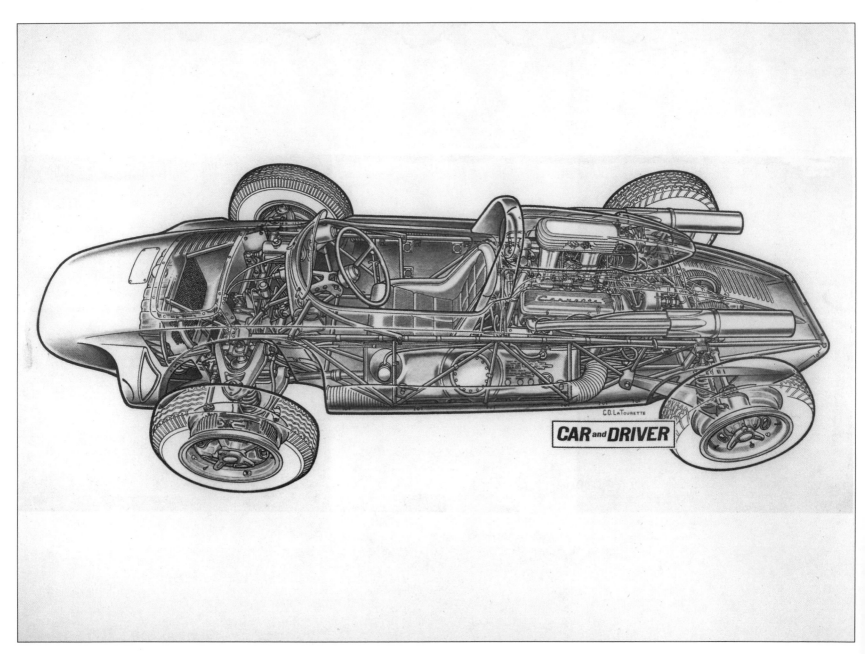

Zora Duntov was able to use many spare Corvette SS chassis components when he built the CERV I in 1960. It was one of the first racing cars to use rubber aircraft-type bag tanks to carry its fuel supply.

Larry Shinoda styled the racy lines of the CERV I, nicknamed the "Hillclimber" because Zora hoped to use it to set a new record at Pike's Peak, Colorado. Duntov had broken the production-car record there with the 1956 Chevrolet.

An advanced rear suspension for the CERV I was designed by Zora, Harold Krieger, and Walt Zetye. Each hub was guided by a trailing arm and two lateral links, one of which was the drive shaft itself.

The all-aluminum fuel-injected V-8 engine sat well forward in the CERV I because the four-speed gearbox was between it and the rear axle. The long ram pipes of the injection unit gave excellent mid-range torque.

The man and his creation: Zora with CERV I in its 1962 configuration with a cowl-mounted tachometer. In this form it lapped Daytona at 167 mph.

Zora at speed with CERV I. With an altered nose and a 377-cubic-inch V-8, Zora averaged 206 mph with this car around GM's high-speed track at Milford, Michigan in 1964.

PRESLEY
11-18-57

17504

At the end of 1957, designers in GM's Research Studio were preparing all-new body shapes for a radically-transformed 1960 Corvette.

A "space buck" for the proposed 1960 Corvette made room for a rear-mounted transaxle and independent rear suspension, components borrowed from a planned mainstream car program.

Compared with a 1958 Corvette, the Research Studio proposal for 1960 was a much lower and lighter vehicle. Many years later its transaxle configuration would be adopted by the Corvette.

Late in 1963 a GM Styling team under Henry Haga prepared this future Corvette proposal. Its sophisticated lines included side-mounted exhaust pipes.

The 1963 Haga design proposal included doors that swung up and forward around the center pillar of the windshield. An alternative exhaust-pipe design is shown.

MAULER 1-8-62 30547

A 1962 design proposal had racy lines that were more Turin than Detroit. It had nostrils at the front that suggested a possible Pontiac affiliation.

Given the impetus of both the Corvair and Zora's rear-engined CERV I, stylists tried their hand at a rear-engined Corvette design as early as February 1960. Substantial air scoops indicated a rear-mounted radiator.

As project XP-720, design work on the car that became the 1963 Corvette was under way in 1959. This early effort was essentially the racing Sting Ray with a coupe top.

MADLER
9-6-60

30283

By September 1960 the lines of the final Stingray were beginning to emerge. A convertible is assessed on a turntable in the Styling Staff viewing courtyard.

A three-eighths-scale model of the 1963 Corvette was thoroughly evaluated in both coupe and convertible versions in the wind tunnel of the California Institute of Technology under the direction of Dr. Peter Kyropoulos.

The two cars were different in every detail, but there was no denying the family relationship between the racing Sting Ray and the 1963 production Stingray Corvette with its controversial split rear window.

The Stingray that never was – the stretched version of the car with rear seating, as requested by Chevrolet chief Ed Cole.

Its added rear seats clearly visible, the stretched coupe never entered production because the demand for the standard Stingray was overwhelming.

In order to have a road car that would foreshadow the coming shape of the 1963 Corvette, Bill Mitchell, with Larry Shinoda, styled the flamboyant Shark concept car.

MADLER
4-12-61

33644

The spectacular lines of the Shark are seen in April 1961 in the basement studio against a background of Larry Shinoda sketches. The skills of GM's clay modelers were exceptional.

When Zora Duntov decided in 1962 to build a "light" Corvette, Chevrolet's own prototype shop made its ultra-thin fiberglass body.

The engine intended for the Corvette Grand Sport, as it became known, had hemispherical combustion chambers and dual ignition. This rendering was intended to convince the FIA homologation experts that the engine already existed. Although built, it never powered a Grand Sport.

Grand Sport chassis number 1 shows off its aluminum differential housing, carrying a transverse leaf spring, and its disc brakes. These would later be given thicker ventilated discs.

Britain's Girling supplied the Grand Sport's disc brakes. Careful design for production of the 100 planned cars shows in the detail of the frame and parallel-wishbone front suspension.

Chevrolet's intended Cobra-eater, the Grand Sport, was built for lightness and stiffness throughout. At 1,900 pounds it was 37 percent lighter than the production Stingray.

A fuel-injected Corvette engine was installed in the first Grand Sport, whose body is lurking in the background. Heads, block, bell housing, and the transmission housing were all made of aluminum.

The first Corvette Grand Sport poses in the hallway at Chevrolet Engineering outside the room in which it was designed and built. Although ultra-light, it was a faithful replica of the standard car.

Running unofficially after the program was cancelled, a Grand Sport was driven by Dick Thompson at Marlboro, Maryland in April 1963. It was too new to perform at its best.

For an intended entry at Daytona in 1964, two of the Grand Sports were re-bodied as roadsters. Wheelhouse extensions allowed wider tires.

One Grand Sport roadster was acquired by Philadelphian George Wintersteen, who raced it in SCCA events in 1966. Here he is competing at Bridgehampton.

We are back in GM Styling Staff's basement studio in late 1963, looking at the body designed by Larry Shinoda and Tony Lapine for Zora's four-wheel-drive CERV II.

The CERV II was planned as a long-distance racing car to counter the challenge from the GT40 that Ford built after its failure to buy Ferrari. Bunky Knudsen was running Chevrolet then and he didn't want to take second place to anyone.

A single overhead camshaft on each cylinder bank operated the inclined overhead valves of the 377-cubic-inch all-aluminum V-8, designed and built to power the CERV II. It never had a chance to strut its stuff.

Built expressly for racing, CERV II had its driving position on the right. The central tunnel was needed for the drive shaft that went forward from the engine to drive the front differential through a torque converter and two-speed gearbox.

Visible at the lower left is the Corvair torque converter through which the front wheels of the CERV II were driven. The drive shaft to the left front wheel is also shown.

The rear wheels of the CERV II were driven through a Powerglide torque converter and a two-speed gearbox like the one used in the Chaparral sports-racing cars. Here a carbureted Mark IV big-block engine is fitted.

An advanced feature of the CERV II for 1964 was its use of the engine as a major element of the rear of the chassis. However, because the engine was not designed for this use, it had to be supplemented by a tubular structure.

Initially equipped with a 377-cubic-inch Chevrolet V-8, the CERV II reached 200 mph in tests at GM's Milford Proving Ground. It was also tested against the current Chaparral at Jim Hall's Rattlesnake Raceway in 1964.

With its unique four-wheel-drive configuration, the CERV II would have enjoyed a major advantage over all its opposition in endurance racing, which often experiences difficult weather conditions.

Although it was not needed for low-speed operation, the CERV II was equipped with a rear spoiler (not shown) to give it the stability it needed at high track speed.

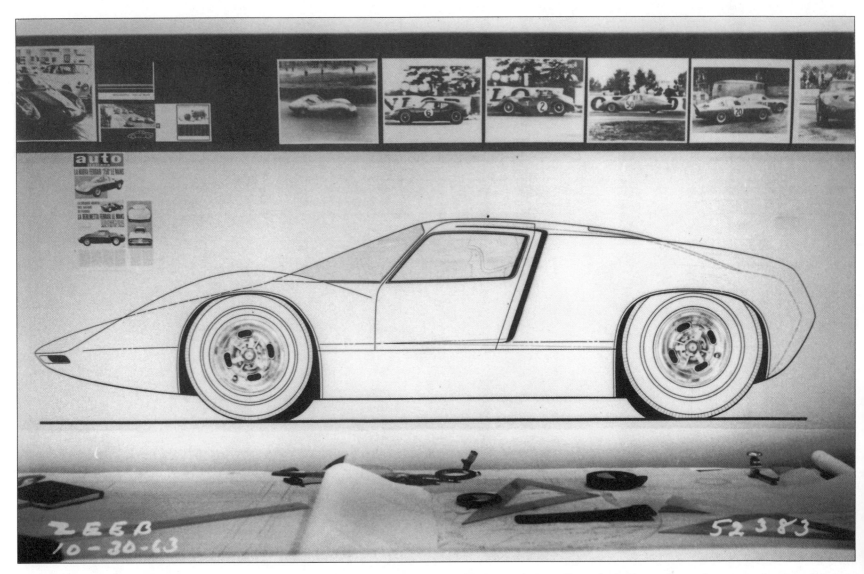

Conceived as it was for endurance racing, the CERV II would have been fitted with a closed coupe body. A tape drawing of October 1963 shows its planned configuration compared to those of other current competition coupes.

With its generous air scoops at the sides of the cockpit, in coupe form the CERV II would have been a striking endurance racer. In the summer of 1964, however, GM decided that it didn't want the bow tie to offer a direct challenge to the blue oval.

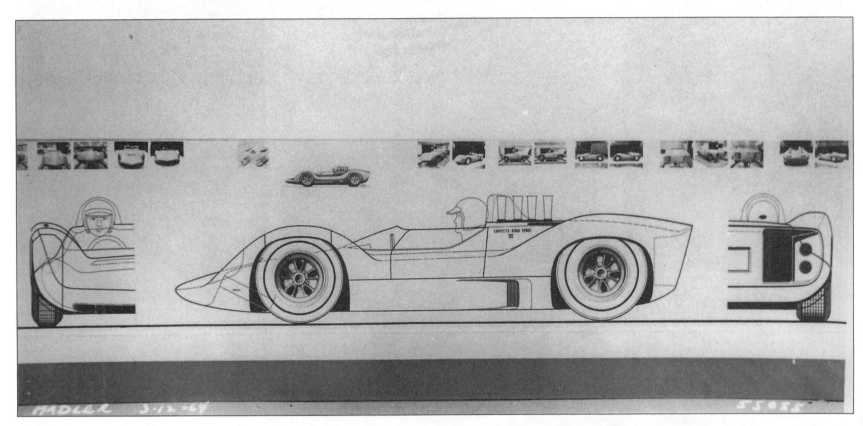

For an experimental racing-car chassis being built by Jim Musser at Chevrolet Engineering, Larry Shinoda designed this low-slung body in March 1964. Its radiator was mounted nearly horizontally.

Jim Musser is attaching test instrumentation to the Chevrolet GS-2b sports-racing car. It faithfully interpreted the Shinoda design.

At the GM Milford Proving Ground, Musser buckles up before trying the capabilities of the GS-2b. Its all-aluminum monocoque frame was adopted for racing in 1965 by the Chaparral team.

Musser accelerates away in the GS-2b. It was built to test both frame and suspension components to help Chevrolet understand the type of componentry that would be needed by a light, European-style sports vehicle.

The concept of a closed version of the Grand Sport 2b was also explored by the GM designers. In 1966 Chaparral would build its own closed version for long-distance racing.

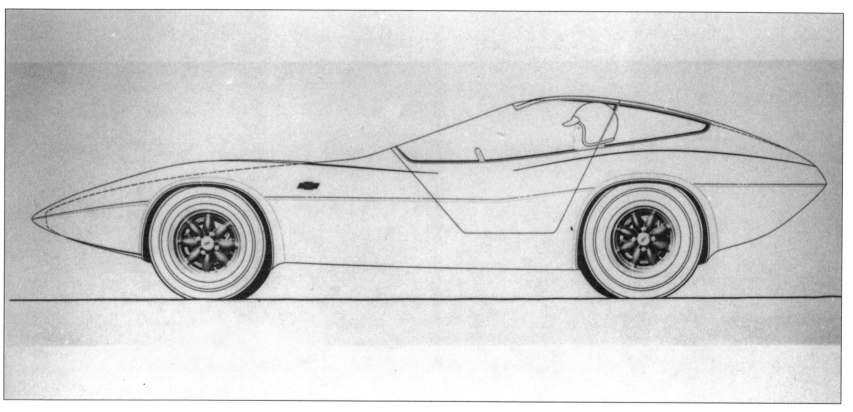

Apart from the Chevrolet bow tie on its flanks, this mid-1960s proposal gives no clue to its purpose. It suggests a smaller and lighter car than the V-8-powered racers that Chevrolet was then building.

Equipped with American Racing aluminum wheels and Goodyear high-performance tires, this is the test vehicle used by Chevrolet for the development of competition components for the new 1969 model Corvette.

Zora peers out of the window of an early prototype of the 1969 Corvette, with its highly-provisional body panels and unusual door handles. Outside exhausts are taken for granted.

A dramatic new offering for 1969 was the aluminum-block version of the big Corvette V-8, the ZL-1. It produced 585 bhp at 6,600 rpm.

Even with the iron-block L88 engine of 427 cubic inches, the 1969 Corvette was no sluggard. This L88 prototype is equipped with special wheels and off-road exhaust pipes.

In 1965 Zora and his engineers were preparing plans for a mid-engined production Corvette. These body shapes were designed to clothe the initial running prototypes.

Duntov's designers proposed in 1965 that the future mid-engined Corvette would have had its radiator mounted in the rear. Roof sections were planned to be removable.

To clothe the 1965 mid-engined chassis, the designers at Styling Staff proposed a much more radical shape, which would have provided rear vision solely through a periscope.

The mid-engined Corvette design proposal from Styling, completed in March 1966, had bold air intakes at the rear and a split windscreen that lifted up with the wide gullwing doors.

Working under Frank Winchell in Chevrolet Engineering's R&D Department, Larry Nies was responsible for the design of a potential mid-engine production Corvette. He reversed the engine in the chassis to place its water pump near the rear-mounted radiator.

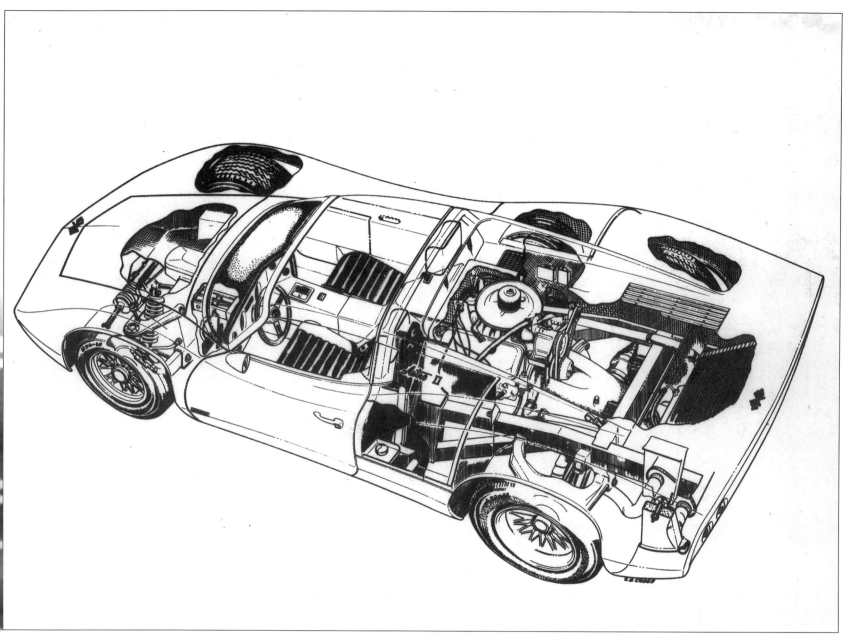

Completed in February 1968, the Nies R&D prototype was known as the XP-880 from its Styling Staff designation. It made use of production chassis components to the extent practicable.

Although easily accessible when the door was opened, seating in the XP-880 was very snug – too much so for some drivers. Nevertheless it gave very good support in cornering.

The XP-880 used a steel backbone-type frame, which split like a tuning fork at the rear to embrace the engine. The fuel tank was installed in the central backbone.

Although not built or intended for external display, the experimental XP-880 was spruced up and renamed "Astro II" for display at the New York Show in April 1968. This was another skirmish in the mid-engine-car battle between Ford and Chevrolet.

The XP-880 used an automatic transmission based on that of the Pontiac Tempest. Its road wheels had the new laced pattern that Chevrolet Engineering had developed for use by Jim Hall's racing Chaparrals.

Zora Duntov's team developed the XP-882 mid-engine Corvette prototype in the 1968-1969 period as a rival to the XP-880. Like the latter it used an automatic transmission, but in an unique layout that provided for future four-wheel drive.

Again, like the XP-880, the XP-882 was primped at the last minute for an appearance at the New York Show in April 1970. It kept Ford from hogging all the limelight with its De Tomaso Pantera.

New aluminum wheels made their first appearance in 1970 on the XP-882. Their classic looks led to them being offered for the production Corvettes as well.

By placing the V-8 engine transversely just ahead of the rear wheels, Zora and his engineers gave the XP-882 the compact wheelbase of 95.5 inches. The lack of a suitable manual transaxle, however, deterred Chevrolet from initiating its production.

With its "Chevrolet GT" program initiated in 1971, GM Design Staff (as it had been renamed) aimed to create a compact two-seater with the potential to be a world sports car, appealing equally to owners of Corvettes and the late lamented Opel GT.

Emerging in 1973 as the 2-Rotor concept car, the Chevrolet GT was a delightfully crisp vehicle whose dimensions were close to those of the Ferrari Dino 246GT.

Space for stowage was available both front and rear in the 2-Rotor prototype. Unusually, GM Design accepted existing American Racing aluminum wheels for their prototype.

Designed with production in mind, the 2-Rotor met all legal requirements for safety and bumper protection. Initially silver, as fabricated by Pininfarina, it was repainted red for its public debut at Frankfurt in September 1973.

Tucked in the engine bay of the 2-Rotor was one of GM's experimental Wankel rotary engines, obviously containing two triangular rotors. It developed 180 bhp and could easily have been tuned to achieve 250 bhp.

As built, the prototype Corvette 2-Rotor had a 3-speed automatic transmission. Designs had also been prepared for an appropriate 4-speed transverse manual gearbox; this would have been needed in any case by the front-drive sedans in which the engine was also to be used.

The elegant lines of the Corvette 2-Rotor had a distinctly European touch. Its potential for world sales would have been high with or without its controversial rotary engine.

Although it was perhaps the 2-Rotor's least-successful element, the styling of its front end was echoed by the later Chevrolet Monza. John De Lorean tried to win GM's permission to build the 2-Rotor as a sports car of his own after leaving GM.

The same XP-882 that had been shown in New York in 1970 served as the basis for the Corvette 4-Rotor prototype of 1973. Under Bill Mitchell, Henry Haga was responsible for its sweeping lines.

With its windscreen sloped at 72 degrees, the 4-Rotor attacked the air like an eager jet plane. Here its clay model is trimmed for evaluation.

Testing of the three-eighths-scale model of the 4-Rotor in the California Institute of Technology tunnel (compare with page 56) showed its drag coefficient to be 0.325, low for 1973. The rear compartment ducting was fully simulated.

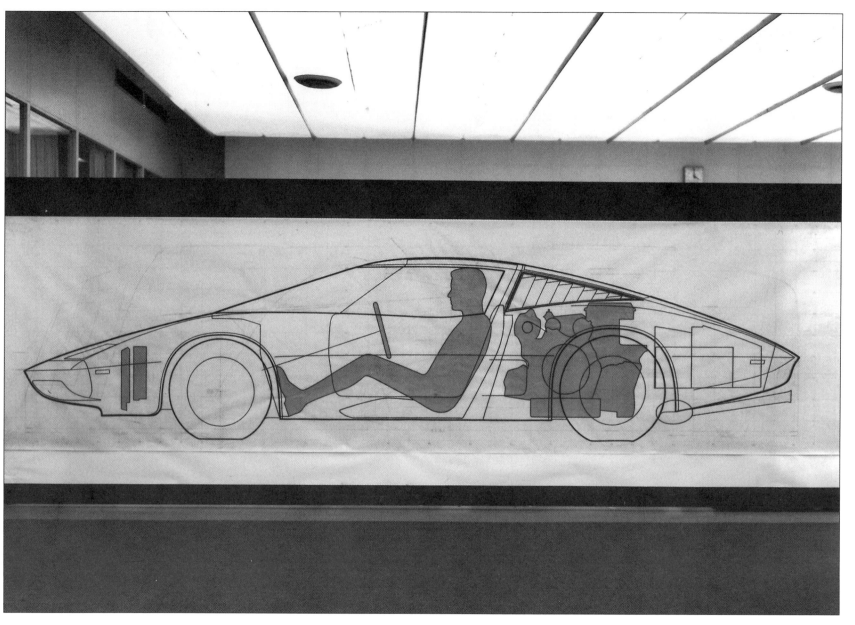

By combining two GM two-rotor Wankel engines, Gib Hufstader created a 4-rotor engine placed transversely behind the seats. Its drive system made use of the main elements of the power train of the XP-882.

The design by Henry Haga featured transparent glass louvers for the engine room and an exceptionally long, low tapered rear deck. The new-look wheels of the XP-882 were judged good enough to remain.

Admirably clean-lined, the 4-Rotor Corvette concept car suffered an interruption to its front deck only when the headlamp units were raised. The radiator was front-mounted.

Between the car's two 2-rotor engines, a cogged rubber belt drove the oil pump, the alternator, and a special distributor. With 48.75 cubic inches in each of its chambers, it was the largest rotary engine ever installed in a vehicle. Its output was some 350 bhp at 7,000 rpm.

An exceptionally elegant feature of an elegant design was the bi-fold gullwing door arrangement of the 4-Rotor. The lower door section automatically folded inward as the door was raised. It made no provision for opening side glass.

Visitors to the Paris Salon in October 1973 had the pleasure of seeing the brand-new Corvette 4-Rotor, Zora's macho rejoinder to the less aggressive statement made by the 2-Rotor prototype.

Paris in October 1973 – just 20 years have passed since the showing there of the original Corvette. They were, to say the least, two very busy and adventurous decades.

More Titles from Iconografix:

AMERICAN CULTURE

AMERICAN SERVICE STATIONS 1935-1943 PHOTO ARCHIVE .... ISBN 1-882256-27-1
COCA-COLA: A HISTORY IN PHOTOGRAPHS 1930-1969 .... ISBN 1-882256-46-8
COCA-COLA: ITS VEHICLES IN PHOTOGRAPHS 1930-1969 .... ISBN 1-882256-47-6
PHILLIPS 66 1945-1954 PHOTO ARCHIVE .... ISBN 1-882256-42-5

AUTOMOTIVE

CADILLAC 1948-1964 PHOTO ALBUM .... ISBN 1-882256-83-2
CORVETTE THE EXOTIC EXPERIMENTAL CARS, LUDVIGSEN LIBRARY SERIES .... ISBN 1-58388-017-8
CORVETTE PROTOTYPES & SHOW CARS PHOTO ALBUM .... ISBN 1-882256-77-8
EARLY FORD V-8S 1932-1942 PHOTO ALBUM .... ISBN 1-882256-97-2
IMPERIAL 1955-1963 PHOTO ARCHIVE .... ISBN 1-882256-22-0
IMPERIAL 1964-1968 PHOTO ARCHIVE .... ISBN 1-882256-23-9
LINCOLN MOTOR CARS 1920-1942 PHOTO ARCHIVE .... ISBN 1-882256-57-3
LINCOLN MOTOR CARS 1946-1960 PHOTO ARCHIVE .... ISBN 1-882256-58-1
PACKARD MOTOR CARS 1935-1942 PHOTO ARCHIVE .... ISBN 1-882256-44-1
PACKARD MOTOR CARS 1946-1958 PHOTO ARCHIVE .... ISBN 1-882256-45-X
PONTIAC DREAM CARS, SHOW CARS & PROTOTYPES 1928-1998 PHOTO ALBUM .... ISBN 1-882256-93-X
PONTIAC FIREBIRD TRANS-AM 1969-1999 PHOTO ALBUM .... ISBN 1-882256-95-6
PORSCHE 356 1948-1965 PHOTO ALBUM .... ISBN 1-882256-85-9
STUDEBAKER 1933-1942 PHOTO ARCHIVE .... ISBN 1-882256-24-7
STUDEBAKER 1946-1958 PHOTO ARCHIVE .... ISBN 1-882256-25-5

EMERGENCY VEHICLES

AMERICAN LAFRANCE 700 SERIES 1945-1952 PHOTO ARCHIVE .... ISBN 1-882256-90-5
AMERICAN LAFRANCE 700 & 800 SERIES 1953-1958 PHOTO ARCHIVE .... ISBN 1-882256-91-3
AMERICAN LAFRANCE 900 SERIES 1958-1964 PHOTO ARCHIVE .... ISBN 1-58388-002-X
CLASSIC AMERICAN AMBULANCES 1900-1979 PHOTO ARCHIVE .... ISBN 1-882256-94-8
CLASSIC AMERICAN FUNERAL VEHICLES 1900-1980 PHOTO ARCHIVE .... ISBN 1-58388-016-X
FIRE CHIEF CARS 1900-1997 PHOTO ALBUM .... ISBN 1-882256-87-5
LOS ANGELES CITY FIRE APPARATUS 1953 - 1999 PHOTO ALBUM .... ISBN 1-58388-012-7
MACK® MODEL B FIRE TRUCKS 1954-1966 PHOTO ARCHIVE* .... ISBN 1-882256-62-X
MACK MODEL C FIRE TRUCKS 1957-1967 PHOTO ARCHIVE* .... ISBN 1-58388-014-3
MACK MODEL CF FIRE TRUCKS 1967-1981 PHOTO ARCHIVE* .... ISBN 1-882256-63-8
MACK MODEL L FIRE TRUCKS 1940-1954 PHOTO ARCHIVE* .... ISBN 1-882256-86-7
PIERCE ARROW FIRE APPARATUS 1979-1998 PHOTO ARCHIVE .... ISBN 1-58388-023-2
SEAGRAVE 70TH ANNIVERSARY SERIES PHOTO ARCHIVE .... ISBN 1-58388-001-1
VOLUNTEER & RURAL FIRE APPARATUS PHOTO GALLERY .... ISBN 1-58388-005-4

RACING

GT40 PHOTO ARCHIVE .... ISBN 1-882256-64-6
INDY CARS OF THE 1950s, LUDVIGSEN LIBRARY SERIES .... ISBN 1-58388-018-6
JUAN MANUEL FANGIO WORLD CHAMPION DRIVER SERIES PHOTO ALBUM .... ISBN 1-58388-008-9
LE MANS 1950: THE BRIGGS CUNNINGHAM CAMPAIGN PHOTO ARCHIVE .... ISBN 1-882256-21-2
LOTUS RACE CARS 1961-1994 PHOTO ALBUM .... ISBN 1-882256-84-0
MARIO ANDRETTI WORLD CHAMPION DRIVER SERIES PHOTO ALBUM .... ISBN 1-58388-009-7
SEBRING 12-HOUR RACE 1970 PHOTO ARCHIVE .... ISBN 1-882256-20-4
VANDERBILT CUP RACE 1936 & 1937 PHOTO ARCHIVE .... ISBN 1-882256-66-2
WILLIAMS 1969-1998 30 YEARS OF GRAND PRIX RACING PHOTO ALBUM .... ISBN 1-58388-000-3

RAILWAYS

CHICAGO, ST. PAUL, MINNEAPOLIS & OMAHA RAILWAY 1880-1940 PHOTO ARCHIVE ...... ISBN 1-882256-67-0
CHICAGO & NORTH WESTERN RAILWAY 1975-1995 PHOTO ARCHIVE .... ISBN 1-882256-76-X
GREAT NORTHERN RAILWAY 1945-1970 PHOTO ARCHIVE .... ISBN 1-882256-56-5
GREAT NORTHERN RAILWAY 1945-1970 VOL 2 PHOTO ARCHIVE .... ISBN 1-882256-79-4
MILWAUKEE ROAD 1850-1960 PHOTO ARCHIVE .... ISBN 1-882256-61-1
SOO LINE 1975-1992 PHOTO ARCHIVE .... ISBN 1-882256-68-9
TRAINS OF THE TWIN PORTS, DULUTH-SUPERIOR IN THE 1950s PHOTO ARCHIVE .... ISBN 1-58388-003-8
TRAINS OF THE CIRCUS 1872-1956 PHOTO ARCHIVE .... ISBN 1-58388-024-0
WISCONSIN CENTRAL LIMITED 1987-1996 PHOTO ARCHIVE .... ISBN 1-882256-75-1
WISCONSIN CENTRAL RAILWAY 1871-1909 PHOTO ARCHIVE .... ISBN 1-882256-78-6

TRUCKS & BUSES

BEVERAGE TRUCKS 1910-1975 PHOTO ARCHIVE .... ISBN 1-882256-60-3
BROCKWAY TRUCKS 1948-1961 PHOTO ARCHIVE* .... ISBN 1-882256-55-7
DODGE PICKUPS 1939-1978 PHOTO ALBUM .... ISBN 1-882256-82-4
DODGE POWER WAGONS 1940-1980 PHOTO ARCHIVE .... ISBN 1-882256-89-1
DODGE POWER WAGON PHOTO HISTORY .... ISBN 1-58388-019-4
DODGE TRUCKS 1929-1947 PHOTO ARCHIVE .... ISBN 1-882256-36-0
DODGE TRUCKS 1948-1960 PHOTO ARCHIVE .... ISBN 1-882256-37-9
THE GENERAL MOTORS NEW LOOK BUS PHOTO ARCHIVE .... ISBN 1-58388-007-0
JEEP 1941-2000 PHOTO ARCHIVE .... ISBN 1-58388-021-6
LOGGING TRUCKS 1915-1970 PHOTO ARCHIVE .... ISBN 1-882256-59-X
MACK MODEL AB PHOTO ARCHIVE* .... ISBN 1-882256-18-2
MACK AP SUPER-DUTY TRUCKS 1926-1938 PHOTO ARCHIVE* .... ISBN 1-882256-54-9
MACK BUSES 1900-1960 PHOTO ARCHIVE* .... ISBN 1-58388-020-8
MACK MODEL B 1953-1966 VOL 1 PHOTO ARCHIVE* .... ISBN 1-882256-19-0
MACK MODEL B 1953-1966 VOL 2 PHOTO ARCHIVE* .... ISBN 1-882256-34-4
MACK EB-EC-ED-EE-EF-EG-DE 1936-1951 PHOTO ARCHIVE* .... ISBN 1-882256-29-8
MACK EH-EJ-EM-EQ-ER-ES 1936-1950 PHOTO ARCHIVE* .... ISBN 1-882256-39-5
MACK FC-FCSW-NW 1936-1947 PHOTO ARCHIVE* .... ISBN 1-882256-28-X
MACK FG-FH-FJ-FK-FN-FP-FT-FW 1937-1950 PHOTO ARCHIVE* .... ISBN 1-882256-35-2
MACK LF-LH-LJ-LM-LT 1940-1956 PHOTO ARCHIVE* .... ISBN 1-882256-38-7
MACK TRUCKS PHOTO GALLERY* .... ISBN 1-882256-88-3
NEW CAR CARRIERS 1910-1998 PHOTO ALBUM .... ISBN 1-882256-98-0
PLYMOUTH COMMERCIAL VEHICLES PHOTO ARCHIVE .... ISBN 1-58388-004-6
STUDEBAKER TRUCKS 1927-1940 PHOTO ARCHIVE .... ISBN 1-882256-40-9
STUDEBAKER TRUCKS 1941-1964 PHOTO ARCHIVE .... ISBN 1-882256-41-7
WHITE TRUCKS 1900-1937 PHOTO ARCHIVE .... ISBN 1-882256-80-8

TRACTORS & CONSTRUCTION EQUIPMENT

CASE TRACTORS 1912-1959 PHOTO ARCHIVE .... ISBN 1-882256-32-8
CATERPILLAR PHOTO GALLERY .... ISBN 1-882256-70-0
CATERPILLAR POCKET GUIDE THE TRACK-TYPE TRACTORS 1925-1957 .... ISBN 1-58388-022-4
CATERPILLAR D-2 & R-2 PHOTO ARCHIVE .... ISBN 1-882256-99-9
CATERPILLAR D-8 1933-1974 INCLUDING DIESEL 75 & RD-8 PHOTO ARCHIVE ..... ISBN 1-882256-96-4
CATERPILLAR MILITARY TRACTORS VOLUME 1 PHOTO ARCHIVE .... ISBN 1-882256-16-6
CATERPILLAR MILITARY TRACTORS VOLUME 2 PHOTO ARCHIVE .... ISBN 1-882256-17-4
CATERPILLAR SIXTY PHOTO ARCHIVE .... ISBN 1-882256-05-0
CATERPILLAR TEN INCLUDING 7C FIFTEEN & HIGH FIFTEEN PHOTO ARCHIVE ...... ISBN 1-58388-011-9
CATERPILLAR THIRTY 2ND ED. INC. BEST THIRTY, 6G THIRTY & R-4 PHOTO ARCHIVE ...... ISBN 1-58388-006-2
CLETRAC AND OLIVER CRAWLERS PHOTO ARCHIVE .... ISBN 1-882256-43-3
ERIE SHOVEL PHOTO ARCHIVE .... ISBN 1-882256-69-7
FARMALL CUB PHOTO ARCHIVE .... ISBN 1-882256-71-9
FARMALL F- SERIES PHOTO ARCHIVE .... ISBN 1-882256-02-6
FARMALL MODEL H PHOTO ARCHIVE .... ISBN 1-882256-03-4
FARMALL MODEL M PHOTO ARCHIVE .... ISBN 1-882256-15-8
FARMALL REGULAR PHOTO ARCHIVE .... ISBN 1-882256-14-X
FARMALL SUPER SERIES PHOTO ARCHIVE .... ISBN 1-882256-49-2
FORDSON 1917-1928 PHOTO ARCHIVE .... ISBN 1-882256-33-6
HART-PARR PHOTO ARCHIVE .... ISBN 1-882256-08-5
HOLT TRACTORS PHOTO ARCHIVE .... ISBN 1-882256-10-7
INTERNATIONAL TRACTRACTOR PHOTO ARCHIVE .... ISBN 1-882256-48-4
INTERNATIONAL TD CRAWLERS 1933-1962 PHOTO ARCHIVE .... ISBN 1-882256-72-7
JOHN DEERE MODEL A PHOTO ARCHIVE .... ISBN 1-882256-12-3
JOHN DEERE MODEL B PHOTO ARCHIVE .... ISBN 1-882256-01-8
JOHN DEERE MODEL D PHOTO ARCHIVE .... ISBN 1-882256-00-X
JOHN DEERE 30 SERIES PHOTO ARCHIVE .... ISBN 1-882256-13-1
MINNEAPOLIS-MOLINE U-SERIES PHOTO ARCHIVE .... ISBN 1-882256-07-7
OLIVER TRACTORS PHOTO ARCHIVE .... ISBN 1-882256-09-3
RUSSELL GRADERS PHOTO ARCHIVE .... ISBN 1-882256-11-5
TWIN CITY TRACTOR PHOTO ARCHIVE .... ISBN 1-882256-06-9

*This product is sold under license from Mack Trucks, Inc. Mack is a registered Trademark of Mack Trucks, Inc. All rights reserved.

All Iconografix books are available from direct mail specialty book dealers and bookstores worldwide, or can be ordered from the publisher. For book trade and distribution information or to add your name to our mailing list contact:
Iconografix, PO Box 446, Hudson, Wisconsin, 54016   Telephone: (715) 381-9755, (800) 289-3504 (USA), Fax: (715) 381-9756

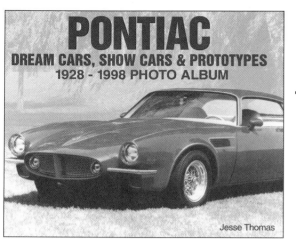
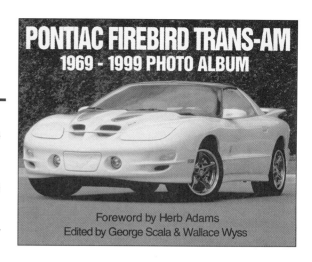
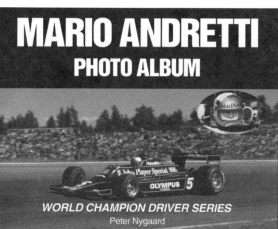

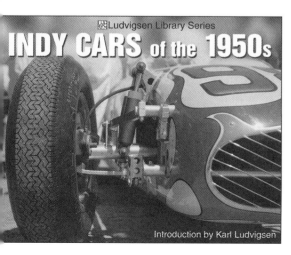
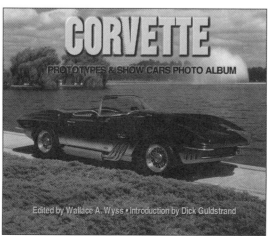
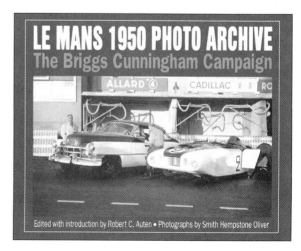

LUDVIGSEN LIBRARY LIMITED

The photographs in this book, supplied by the Ludvigsen Library, are available to purchase. Based in London, this extensive automotive library, founded and owned by Karl Ludvigsen, is one of the world's most comprehensive sources of reference material about cars and the motor industry. Specialising in car and motor racing photography, it includes much rare and unpublished original material from John Dugdale, Edward Eves, Max Le Grand, Peter Keen, Karl Ludvigsen, Rodolfo Mailander, Ove Nielsen, Stanley Rosenthall, and others.

All black and white prints are hand finished to museum display standards using the finest Ilford 1K fibre which gives a beautiful, durable finish that is perfect for mounting and display. Prints can be ordered from the Ludvigsen Library at the address below in three sizes at the following prices:

10 x 12	inches	US$40.00	UK£25.00
12 x 16	inches	US$55.00	UK£35.00
16 x 20	inches	US$75.00	UK£45.00

Please inquire concerning color, other sizes, and other subjects. Prices do not include packing and shipping fees, which will be advised in advance.

THE LUDVIGSEN LIBRARY LIMITED: 73 COLLIER STREET, LONDON N1 9BE, UNITED KINGDOM
TELEPHONE +44 (020) 7837 1700 FACSIMILE +44 (020) 7837 1776
E-MAIL LIBRARY@LUDVIGSEN.COM   HTTP://WWW.LUDVIGSEN.COM